Soft Selling in a Hard World

Sales Manager's Guide

Jerry Vass and Iris Herrin

Books by VASS Publishing:

Soft Selling in a Hard World, 2 Ed—Jerry Vass

Soft Selling to Executives—Jerry Vass and Iris Herrin

Selling in America—*The above books in one volume*

Other books by Jerry Vass:

Sleeping Big in Smallville, a Telluride Story

Just My Luck

All available at *amazon.com*

The
Soft Selling in a Hard World®
Sales Manager's Guide

Copyright 2010-2021 VASS

All rights reserved under the
Pan-American and International Copyright Conventions

This book may not be reproduced in whole or in part in any form or by any means, electronic or mechanical, including photocopying, recording, or by any information storage and retrieval system now known or hereafter invented, without written permission from the publisher.

VASS®, *Soft Selling in a Hard World*® and *Soft Sell*® are registered trade or service marks of the Vass Company.

Vass Training Group
1093 A1A Beach Blvd, Box 448
St. Augustine, FL 32080
www.vass.com

Table of Contents

For teaching purposes, permission is here by granted to reproduce all or parts of this copyrighted material.

Foreword

Persuasion is a process. Sales training is behavior modification.

The mission of this program is to help you radically re-engineer your sales presentation to work from the Buyer's point of view and increase sales 25% or more.

By redefining and redesigning the persuasion process you will find selling no longer filled with mystery but an ongoing, rather simple process of day-to-day business.

This training program combines your business expertise and market knowledge with proven selling tactics to produce a selling presentation that works from the Buyer's point of view and builds a custom selling manual for your company.

The Problem

Keeping your salespeople trained is a constant challenge and, without direction, a management nightmare. Most companies train the technical side of their business. They rarely train the persuasion side because there is so little credible information available for the businessperson, sales manager or entrepreneur.

The Solution

Training persuasion skills is an investment in your business. Expect to generate a return. Invest in training time regularly and expect increased sales of 25% or more.

The transient nature of salespeople is legendary. Using the Soft Selling protocols you can archive the street knowledge your salespeople pick up even as you increase their efficiency while they are with you.

This is behavior modification. Using this *Sales Manager's Guide* and the *Soft Selling in a Hard World®, Second Edition* textbook, you will assign reading and writing assignments. Your salespeople will design and write new selling moves and presentations. Then your salespeople will test the new selling moves in real life selling situations. Based on their Buyer's actual responses they then work with you again to revise and refine the selling moves. Then real-life test again. And revise again until you have constructed a presentation that works 80% of the time.

Introduction

This learning program involves discussion, writing, thinking, designing and venturing into the Buyer's mind.

For your salespeople, the sensitive process of thinking like the Buyer can be as valuable as producing the selling manual for your company. Reshaping your technical expertise into a form the Buyer likes requires time, effort and practice.

About time

VASS® training doesn't take your people "off-line." This training is about merging the salesperson's stuff with persuasion skills. Persuasion is their trade. Company's stuff is the medium. When you use weekly sales meetings as the training venue and dedicate as little as 20 minutes per meeting, it can make a significant difference in the way your salespeople act toward Buyers. Sales growth is the reward for your effort. You do not have to borrow or invest new capital, increase staff, open new offices or buy new machinery to increase your revenue stream by 25%, or more.

About effort

No matter how strongly we wish it were otherwise, selling power lies in choosing and using the right words. The more effort expended in designing the words, the greater the results.

The process of moving inside the Buyer's mind requires writing, rewriting and writing some more. Many managers have rewritten some sections a dozen times or more, each time including a refinement developed from real presentations or developing new, experimental words and phrases to move the Seller closer to the Buyer.

The goal of the program is to have fun, experiment, design, redesign, and move into your Buyer's mind. Remember that the creative center of the brain lives right next door to the laugh center. Laugh more—create more. Laugh a lot, think simple, clear thoughts and move out of your world and into the Buyers'.

                    ©Vass 2010-2021

Getting Started

To design a civilized presentation requires background preparation.

1. Browse through the *Soft Selling in a Hard World* text to get a sense of how the lesson plan is laid out.

2. Browse through this *Training Guide* and *you*'ll see that it is designed in sections, each building on the last.

Then, gather your salespeople and budget 40 minutes of your first sales meeting to lay out the process you will follow to build a company selling manual.

The Training Process

Regular study and review help salespeople internalize the moves of a tactical Buyer-response driven presentation. It also encourages management and salespeople to update their real presentations with the tactical moves that actually work on the street.

Homework

The brief weekly homework reading and writing assignments in the textbook prepare your people for the next training meeting. Preparation makes meeting time shorter and more productive for everyone.

Developing proof statements for your product or service takes time and research. They pay big dividends for the salespeople and the company. Do the research. Find the statistics for your business. Ultimately, numbers are all the Buyer remembers from your presentation. The usual seller's "Glories of Us" are quickly forgotten.

Weekly Drill

This program contains an Introduction and 16 training sessions. Role-playing a single selling move for 20 minutes or more at the end of each sales meeting is an easy way to integrate ongoing sales training into everyone's busy schedule.

General Instructions

As a Sales Manager, your responsibilities include being a good teacher. Here are some hints:

- Allow 20 minutes (or more, if feasible) in each sales meeting to review selling moves. Use this *Sales Manager's Guide* and the *Soft Selling in a Hard World® 2nd Ed.* text as a reference for each review section.

- Have salespeople use current situations and prospects whenever possible. Review one move thoroughly during each sales meeting. Gradually, after the Sellers achieve proficiency in a number of moves, ask them to weave several moves together. Continue in this mode until they can perform a full role-play using the <u>Seven Selling Moves</u>.

- Maintain firm control of the discussion. Due to the mix of product knowledge and selling moves, discussions often digress. Use your own judgment but try to limit discussion to the tactical selling move being studied. (Suggestion: If other issues arise, maintain a list of subjects to be discussed after the selling moves section is completed.)

- Keep the exercises simple and instruct the role-players to keep their moves short, simple, clear and to the point.

- Keep role-plays in the first person, present tense. The Seller plays the role as if it were an actual presentation. An occasional reminder like "Please stay in the role," can be helpful.

- Don't let the Seller step out of role to offer asides. Ask for and allow them to proceed uninterrupted. All critiques should occur after the role-play is completed.

- The phrase "I think…" pulls attention away from the Buyer back to the Seller. To discourage the use of "I think…," instruct all participants to snap their fingers whenever the phrase is used. The Buyer's only interest is "What's in this for me?"

- Since there is often a disparity between the way people think and the way they speak, be sure everyone enjoys an opportunity to play roles. Much of the tactical sell revolves around the actual use of correctly prepared words. Thinking about them doesn't ensure their use in a selling situation. Muscle memory in the brain is only developed by actually speaking the part.

                                                    ©Vass 2010-2021

General Instructions (continued)

- Use the Critique Form (located after Class 16). It is helpful in keeping everyone engaged in the exercise.

- Pick the exercises where you feel your salespeople are the weakest. Or, you may pick a series of exercises to fill the time available. Big money earners indicate they role-play every deal, every day.

- To encourage your salespeople to learn the moves and then stay sharp, assign one move to be practiced as much as possible during each day, for instance, Monday is "Mission Statement Day," Tuesday is "Probes Day," etc.

Idea Generation

When ideas begin to flow, here are some rules to keep them flowing:

- List every idea on a blackboard or flip chart as it comes up.

- All ideas are equal and are not edited or commented upon until later. They may be built upon.

- The more ridiculous and funny the idea, the more it is encouraged.

- When the people are dry of ideas, go back and edit the idea list by first deciding which ideas are impossible, unreasonable or too expensive.

- List the remaining ideas from the most possible to the least possible to accomplish.

- List them from the most productive to the least productive.

- Don't fall in or out of love with any idea. There should be no particular reverence for any idea since, in the right environment, humans are capable of producing a limitless number of them on demand. Be careful that ideas from the president don't overwhelm ideas from the stockroom clerk. Managers are often stuck in habit and need a fresh look at what they are doing.

Language Traps

Watch for Seller's language traps.

- KISS—keep the presentation simple—the confused mind always says no.

- But—don't use the word "but." It indicates an argument is on the way.

- Contractions—don't allow sellers to use contractions to direct a favorable answer (wouldn't, shouldn't, oughtn't, etc.).

- Holding the ball—Sellers speak in two-sentence bursts, then probe. Listening is 70% of selling.

- "I"—the word "I" has no place in the presentation. (Especially "I think....").

- Vomiting—Sellers should not vomit their presentation, but probe instead.

- Guessing—Sellers shouldn't guess at the Buyer's problem.

                                                            ©Vass 2010-2021

The Soft Sell®

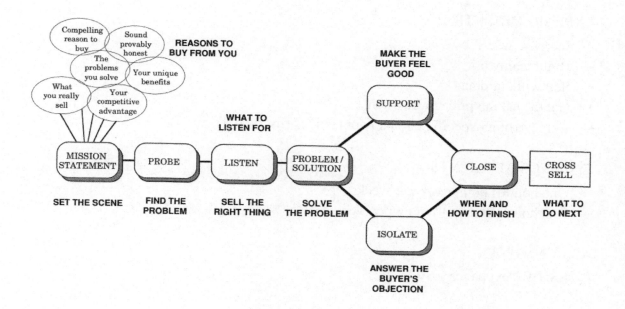

Introduction to Soft Selling in a Hard World®

Class 1——Introduction to *Soft Selling in a Hard World*®

- Schedule one hour with your salespeople.
- Introduce your plan for the training.
- Distribute the *Soft Selling in a Hard World*® textbooks to your salespeople.

EXPLAIN OBJECTIVES

- Increase sales.
- Build teamwork.
- Sell without dread
- Get the asking price more often.
- Achieve other specific company objectives (list below).

TIME COMMITMENTS

- One hour of homework per week.
- One hour of group training per week.

ASSIGNMENT

- SSHW Text pages 1-17.

                    ©Vass 2010-2021

The Easiest Sale™

Class 2—The Soft Sell®

DISCUSS

- the reading assignment—elicit opinions from salespeople and encourage discussion about **Letter from Your Buyer** and **The Easiest Sale**.
- the written assignment—Selling Position.

ASSIGNMENT

- SSHW Text: pages 18-31, 167-170.

Your Business Story

Class 3—60-Second Commercial

> Puffery and Representation.
> Your Business Story.
> Traps.

DISCUSS

- the homework assignment
- the hollowness of the *60-Second Commercia.l*

EXERCISE

- *Puffery and Representation*: Have each person read their differentiating statements
- Combine, edit and refine into a single powerful statement of Representation
- Discuss *Your Business Story* (in 150 words). Combine, edit and refine into a single powerful business story.

WATCH FOR

- What percentage of each statement cannot be proven, that is, Puffery?
- What parts of the statement are proved and therefore are Representation?
- What percentage of each statement sounds exactly like the competition?

ASSIGNMENT

- SSHW Text: pages 53-54; 132-145, 32-39, 197-199.

A Letter from Your Buyer

In a 36-year training career chockablock with surprises, our biggest surprise was that professionals rarely, if ever, look at a sales transaction from the Client's point of view. When espousing the pop psycho-drivel of the day, professionals may conjure "win-win situations" and "sensitive and caring relationships" with their Clients. Galileo could see distant planets only with the help of a telescope. *Soft Selling in a Hard World* and this companion training manual create a telescope to help professionals peer deep into the universe of the buyer's mind.

Your potential and selling power grow out of preparation. This workbook forces you to look at your sales transaction from the Client's point of view and by doing so, sets you apart from your competition, makes you efficient at your work and builds strong personal relationships with your Client. Every exercise is designed to create mutual respect between you and the Client.

The following letter could be from any one of your Clients. It states in plain English what executive level Clients think and feel about salespeople.

If it intimidates or depresses you, it should. This letter indicates how low salespeople rate in the executive's estimation. That low esteem has been well-earned by professionals so poorly trained in selling skills that they're barely able to function as order-takers, let alone persuaders.

This guides exercises allow you to discover that you already know more about your Client's mind than you think, that you hide information that the Client is dying to hear and that you can design a presentation that even "Hatchetman" Johnson, CEO of *United American Global Corporation*, a company with $10 billion in annual global sales, will listen to happily, and then invite you to stay for lunch in the executive dining room.

Mr. Lee Johnson, President
United American Global Corporation

Corporate Center,

Ferndock, New York. 10999

May 32, 2288

Attention, Mr./Ms. Salesperson:

I spend 15% of each day with salespeople. I am trained to listen intently to everything you say, both stated and implied. I hate to watch people waste their valuable time, talent and good intentions. It makes me feel guilty, it bores me, it wastes my time, and it costs me money.

So here are some guidelines for our meeting:

I am adamant that meetings produce tangible results. Please be prepared to give the high points of your proposal in five minutes or less and your entire presentation in 30 minutes or less. Limit your PowerPoint presentation, if any, to seven slides or fewer.

United American International is a performance-based organization. We aren't looking to build overhead functions. We _are_ looking for ways to increase sales, cash flow and profits. We actively seek ways to decrease costs, responsibility, time and labor. Our first level of consciousness is survival, the second level is profits and the third is cash flow.

Applying our criteria, please be prepared to state your objective for this meeting in plain English and in terms of increased sales and/or decreased costs (preferably in dollars), percentages or risk factors.

If our products and services are the subject of the meeting, be advised that everyone has an idea of how our products and services should be changed. We love to hear improvement ideas, but we won't alter our products and services unless you finance the changes. Ours are finished, marketable products and services as they exist.

If you expect us to change our mind just because you want us to, work harder using your methods or plan, give you business without proof of your value or create a friendly environment especially for you, this meeting will be short and considerably tougher for us all.

If you are a profit-oriented, cut-to-the-chase, bottom-line kind of person who wants to look at my problems from my point of view and help me solve them, I'd love to talk to you. The sky is the limit.

Sincerely,

Lee J. Johnson, President

United American Global Corporation

LJJ/cs

     ©Vass 2010-2021

Features and Benefits

Class 4—60-Second Commercial Revisited

The Executive Conversation.
Features and Benefits.

DISCUSS

- 60-Second Commercial Revisited.
- Features and Benefits. Combine, edit and refine for the most powerful.

EXERCISE

- Role-play the four most important Features and Benefits with each person taking a turn playing a Buyer and a Seller. Critique.

WATCH FOR

Did the Seller tie Features and Benefits together?
Was the Seller able to sell Benefits alone?
Did the Seller apply Benefits to the Buyer?
Are you sure the Seller didn't state a Feature followed by another Feature?

REVISIONS

Ask for input from salespeople:
Are there any revisions developed on the street since the last review?
What doesn't work?
What have you found that does work that will improve your presentation?

ASSIGNMENT

- SSHW Text, pages 55-58, 202-203.
- Have salespeople use Benefits with Buyers. Ask salespeople to make notes of Buyer's responses so they may be shared in the next class.

Mission Statements

Class 5—Mission Statements

DISCUSS
- Mission Statements homework. Combine, edit and refine for the three most powerful Mission Statements.

EXERCISE
- Each Seller gives a general Mission Statement for your company.
- In the second round, each Seller gives a Mission Statement using a specific problem and/or specific Buyer.

WATCH FOR
- Is the statement 40 words or less?
- Does it introduce you?
- Does it justify why you are taking up the Buyer's time?
- Does it buy your way in with Benefits?
- Does it contain one compelling Benefit?
- Does it explain your solution to the Buyer's problem?
- Does it explain Features of your product or service? (It shouldn't.)

REVISIONS
Ask for input from salespeople:
- Are there any revisions developed on the street since the last review?
- What doesn't work?
- What have you found that does work that will improve your presentation?

ASSIGNMENT
- SSHW Text: pages 58-76, 206-211.
- Have salespeople use a Mission Statement with Buyers. Ask salespeople to make notes of Buyers' responses so they may be shared and further developed in the next class.

Probes

Class 6—Standard, Status Quo, Best Of All Possible Worlds and Emergency Probes

DISCUSS

- How did Mission Statements work on the street?
- Probes homework. Combine, edit and refine for most powerful yet unassuming probes.

EXERCISE

- Each Seller delivers one Standard, Status Quo, Best Of All Possible Worlds, Emergency Probe.
- In the second round, each Seller delivers a second and different Probe.

WATCH FOR

- Do they flank? (begin with who, how, what, when or where).
- Do they sound intelligent?
- Is the information gathered usable later in the presentation?
- Are they about business rather than products and services?

REVISIONS

Ask for input from salespeople:

- Are there any revisions developed on the street since the last review?
- What doesn't work?
- What have you found that does work that will improve your presentation?

Status Quo Probes

Class 6 (continued)—Status Quo Probes

DISCUSS
- How did Standard probes work on the street?
- Status Quo Probes homework. Combine, edit and refine for the most powerful.

EXERCISE
- Each Seller gives one general Status Quo Probe.
- In the second round, each Seller gives one Status Quo Probe that fits a specific problem or current prospect.

WATCH FOR
- Does the probe attempt to uncover dissatisfactions by making the Buyer carefully assess the current situation?
- Does the probe direct the Buyer to discuss things that are favorable about the present circumstance you are selling against? (It shouldn't).
- Does the probe leave the implication with the Buyer that his or her current situation leaves something to be desired which you can help?
- Does the probe imply bad decision-making by the Buyer? (It shouldn't).
- Does the probe set up a closing move?
- Does the probe attack the competition? (It shouldn't).

REVISIONS
Ask for input from salespeople:
- Are there any revisions developed on the street since the last review?
- What doesn't work?
- What have you found that does work that will improve your presentation?

©Vass 2010-2021

Best-of-All-Possible-Worlds/Emergency Probes

Class 6 (continued)—Best-of-All-Possible-Worlds and Emergency Probes

DISCUSS

- How did Status Quo Probes work on the street?
- Discuss Best-of-All-Possible-Worlds Probes and the Emergency Probe homework.
- Combine, edit and refine for the most powerful.

EXERCISE

- Each Seller gives a Best-of-All-Possible-Worlds Probe.
- Each Seller gives an Emergency Probe.

WATCH FOR

- Does the BOAPW Probe allow the Buyer to dream?
- Does it encourage an expansive answer rather than a restrictive one?
- Does the Emergency Probe place the ball in the Buyer's court?
- Does it buy sufficient time for you to regroup?

REVISIONS

Ask for input from salespeople:

- Are there any revisions developed on the street since the last review?
- What doesn't work?
- What have you found that does work that will improve your presentation?

©Vass 2010-2021

Probes

Class 6 (continued)—Best of Probes Edit

DISCUSS
- Listening skills.

EXERCISE
- Review probes. Combine, edit and refine best in each category.
- Define and discuss the 4 types of probes.
- Going around, have each person give one example each of Standard, Status Quo, Best-of-All-Possible-Worlds and Emergency Probes.

WATCH FOR
- Does each person understand the difference between the types of probes?
- Does each person understand the uses of the different types of probes?
- Was each of the probes Flanking?

REVISIONS

Ask for input from salespeople:
- Are there any revisions developed on the street since the last review?
- What doesn't work?
- What have you found that does work that will improve your presentation?

ASSIGNMENT
- SSHW Text: pages 80-84.

©Vass 2010-2021

Problem/Solution/Benefit

Class 7—Problem/Solution

DISCUSS

- Problem/Solution homework.
- Combine, edit and refine for the most common Buyer's business problems.
- Combine, edit and refine for the most powerful Benefit.
- Determine the Proofs required for your solution.

EXERCISE

- Each Buyer states a business problem or need. Each Seller then forms a Problem/Solution.
- Each Seller probes the Buyer using Flanking Probes to determine the Buyer's business problem or need and then delivers an appropriate Problem/Solution.

WATCH FOR

- Did the Seller state the Buyer's problem first?
- Was the problem stated the real business problem or only a symptom?
- Did the Seller state the solution to the Buyer's problem second?
- Was there a Benefit stated?
- Could the Benefit be proven?
- If used, were the probes flanking?

REVISIONS

Ask for input from salespeople:

- Are there any revisions developed on the street since the last review?
- What doesn't work?
- What have you found that does work that will improve your presentation?

ASSIGNMENT

- SSHW Text: pages 93-109.
- Have salespeople use Problem/Solution/Benefit with Buyers and make notes of Buyers' responses so they may be shared and further developed in the next class.

Objections

Class 8—Objections

DISCUSS

- How did Problem/Solution/Benefit work on the street?
- Discuss homework

EXERCISE

- Role-play answers to four objections (other than Price and Status Quo) that cost you the most business.
- Role-play answers to the most likely objections of your current prospects (other than Price and Status Quo).

WATCH FOR

- Did the Seller answer the Objection in a convincing, provable manner?
- Did the Seller use puffery? [(S)he shouldn't].
- If required, did the Seller use Proof statements?
- Using probes, did the Seller isolate the objection correctly (that is, answer the correct objection)?
- Did the Seller keep the answer simple?
- Were Benefits applied directly to the Buyer?

REVISIONS

Ask for input from salespeople:
- Are there any revisions developed on the street since the last review?
- What doesn't work?
- What have you found that does work that will improve your presentation?

                    ©Vass 2010-2021

Price Objections

Class 8 (continued)—Price Objections

DISCUSS

- How did answers to Objections work on the street?
- Discuss homework

EXERCISE

- Each seller in turn answers a price objection
- Combine, edit and refine the Offsetting Benefits
- Quantify the Offsetting Benefits

WATCH FOR

- Did the Seller answer the Objection in a convincing, provable manner?
- Did the Seller use puffery? [(S)he shouldn't].
- If required, did the Seller use Proof Statements?
- Using probes, did the Seller isolate the objection correctly (that is, answer the correct objection)?
- Did the Seller keep the answer simple?
- Were Benefits applied directly to the Buyer?
- Were the Benefits quantified?

REVISIONS

Ask for input from salespeople:

- Are there any revisions developed on the street since the last review?
- What doesn't work?
- What have you found that does work that will improve your presentation?

ASSIGNMENT

- SSHW Text: pages 40-47.
- Have salespeople use the answers to the Price Objection with their Buyers. Ask salespeople to make notes of Buyers' responses so they may be shared and further developed in the next meeting.

Proof Statements

Class 9—Proof Statements

DISCUSS

- How do answers to the Price Objection work on the street?
- Discuss homework.
- Develop plan for acquiring and identify sources for Proof Statements.

EXERCISE

- Review Proof Statements that are readily available.
- Ask salespeople to suggest Proof Statements that management needs to develop.

WATCH FOR

- Does the Proof Statement quote reputable sources outside your business?
- Does the Proof Statement answer the Buyer's doubt stated or implied in the objection?
- Do the Benefits apply directly to the Buyer?

REVISIONS

Ask for input from salespeople:
- Are there any revisions developed on the street since the last review?
- What doesn't work?
- What have you found that does work that will improve your presentation?

ASSIGNMENT

- SSHW Text: pages 110-118.
- Have salespeople use Proof Statements with Buyers. Ask salespeople to make notes of Buyers' responses so they may be shared and further developed at the next class.

                    ©Vass 2010-2021

Closes

Class 10—Closes

DISCUSS

• How did Proof Statements work on the street?
• Discuss homework.

EXERCISE

• Role-play Closes.

WATCH FOR

• Does the Close acquire technical information required to get the Buyer to use your services?
• Does the Close begin with who, how, what, when or where?
• Does the Close require too big a decision from the Buyer? (It shouldn't.)
• Does the Seller's language reflect an assumption that the sale was made?
• Were qualifying words like "If..." used? (They shouldn't be.)

REVISIONS

Ask for input from salespeople:

• Are there any revisions developed on the street since the last review?
• What doesn't work?
• What have you found that does work that will improve your presentation?

ASSIGNMENT

• SSHW Text: pages 120-128.
• Have salespeople Close Buyers in every transaction. Ask salespeople to make notes of Buyers' responses so they may be shared and further developed at the next class.

©Vass 2010-2021

90-Second Close

Class 11—90-Second Close

DISCUSS
- How do Closes work on the street?
- Discuss homework

EXERCISE
- Role-play 90-Second Close

WATCH FOR
- Did the Seller state Buyer's problem, the solution, the Benefit of the solution and a Probe with a Closing Premise?
- Did the probe elicit a positive response which could be supported and closed?

REVISIONS

Ask for input from salespeople:
- Are there any revisions developed on the street since the last review?
- What doesn't work?
- What have you found that does work that will improve your presentation?

ASSIGNMENT
- SSHW Text: page 119.
- Have salespeople use the 90-Second Close with Buyers in every transaction. Ask salespeople to make notes of Buyers' responses so they may be shared and further developed at the next class.

　　　　　　　　　　　　©Vass 2010-2021

Cross Sell

Class 12—Cross Sell, Skills Test, Soft Sell®

DISCUSS

- How do 90-Second Closes work on the street?
- Discuss homework.

EXERCISE

- Combine, edit and refine Cross Sell opportunities.

WATCH FOR

- Logical progressions from one sell to the next.

REVISIONS

Ask for input from salespeople:

- Are there any revisions developed on the street since the last review?
- What doesn't work?
- What have you found that does work that will improve your presentation?

ASSIGNMENT

- SSHW Text: page 223.
- Have salespeople use the Cross-Sell with Buyers in every transaction. Ask salespeople to make notes of Buyers' responses so they may be shared and further developed at the next class.

Full Role-plays

Class 13—Full Role-plays

DISCUSS

- How does the Cross Sell work on the street?
- Discuss homework

EXERCISE

- Using current prospects and transactions, role-play the full presentation including the most likely objections using the Tactical Presentation homework.

WATCH FOR

- Those elements outlined in the Critique Form (Last page of this manual).

REVISIONS

Ask for input from salespeople:
- Are there any revisions developed on the street since the last review?
- What doesn't work?
- What have you found that does work that will improve your presentation?

ASSIGNMENT

- SSHW Text: pages 154-163.
- Have salespeople use Tactical Presentation forms to prepare for calls with Buyers in every transaction. Ask salespeople to make notes of Buyers' responses so they may be shared and further developed in the next class.

Telephone Presentations

Class 14—Telephone Presentations

DISCUSS

- How does the Tactical Presentation work on the street?
- Discuss homework.

EXERCISE

- Role-play telephone cold calls to get personal appointments.
- Refine cold call language with emphasis on the Mission Statement and Status Quo Probes.

WATCH FOR

- Was the Mission Statement effective?
- Was there an opportunity to Support the Buyer?
- Was there unneeded language used?
- Did the Seller close on the appointment only?

REVISIONS

Ask for input from salespeople:
- Are there any revisions developed on the street since the last review?
- What doesn't work?
- What have you found that does work that will improve your presentation?

ASSIGNMENT

- Have salespeople use the telephone skills with Buyers in every telephone cold call. Ask salespeople to make notes of Buyers' responses so they may be shared and further developed in the next class.

Time Costing

Class 15—Time Costing

DISCUSS

- Discuss homework.

EXERCISE

- Role-play the most important upcoming presentations.

WATCH FOR

- Elements in the Role-play Critique checklist on page 36.

REVISIONS

Ask for input from salespeople:
- Are there any revisions developed on the street since the last review?
- What doesn't work?
- What have you found that does work that will improve your presentation?

ASSIGNMENT

- SSHW Text: pages 182-184.

©Vass 2010-2021

Review

Class 16—Review

Some ideas for keeping this profitable knowledge alive in your company:

- Assign role-play partners, two people that work together to combine, edit and refine the moves on the street and regularly role-play upcoming presentations.

- Encourage role-playing of every major upcoming presentation.

- As a standard practice, use Tactical Presentation forms to prepare every call.

- Keep new workbooks, textbooks and the company selling manual on hand to quickly bring new employees up to speed.

- Take the best of every exercise developed during this training program and build into the company selling manual.

- As the business or market changes because of new products, policies, strategies or market conditions, go back to the workbook and re-design the company selling manual to develop the new selling tactics.

- Schedule at least two hours a month to review and troubleshoot street presentations.

A cautionary note:
This knowledge slips away quickly if not reviewed regularly. While reviews with your salespeople may be a pain to schedule, they pay huge dividends in successful presentations.

Good luck. Good hunting. Good selling.

—Jerry Vass

©Vass 2010-2021

Critique Form

CLASS SUBJECTS	NAME																		DATE
1. Introduction																			
2. Buyer's Letter																			
3. Easiest Sale																			
4. 60-Sec. Commercial																			
5. Features/Benefits																			
6. Value Positions																			
7. Probes																			
8. Problem/Solution																			
9. Objections																			
10. Proof Statements																			
11. Closes																			
12. 90-Second Close																			
13. Cross-Sell																			
14. Full Role-Play																			
15. Phone Presentat'ns																			
16. Proposals																			
17. Ask & Solve																			
18. Time Costing																			
19. Inst. Arrogance																			
20. Review																			

GRADE   5-Excellent   4- Good   3-Fair   2-Poor   1-Find other work

©Vass 2010-2021

Worksheets & Forms

The Selling Conversation

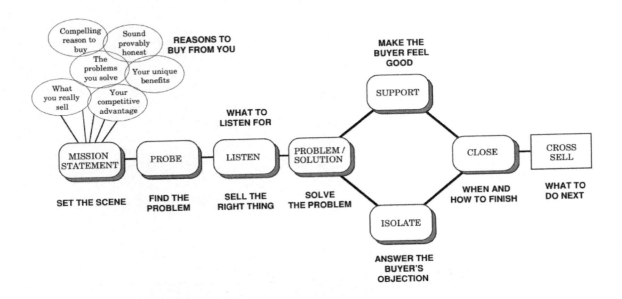

©Vass 2010-2021

Features Advantages Benefits

PROCESS (for the Seller)		RESULTS (for the Client)	
FEATURE	**ADVANTAGE**	**BUSINESS BENEFIT**	**PERSONAL BENEFIT**

©Vass 2010-2021

Features Advantages Benefits

PROCESS (for the Seller)		RESULTS (for the Client)	
FEATURE	**ADVANTAGE**	**BUSINESS BENEFIT**	**PERSONAL BENEFIT**

                                                       ©Vass 2010-2021

Sales Call Preparation Form

Assume your three best competitors are competing for this business. Prepare the following elements of your persuasive dialog with the Buyer:

What is the Buyer's business problem you will most likely uncover?

What is the Buyer's **personal problem** you will most likely uncover?

Develop answers to the questions on this Buyer's mind:

A. *"Why should I spend my time talking to you?"*

What **Mission Statement** with quantifiable benefit will you use?

B. *"Why should I buy from you rather than your competitor?"*

In your selling proposition, what **three key points** do you want this Buyer to remember?
1)

2)

3)

C. *"What makes you different from them?"*

What is your compelling competitive advantage?

D. *"Why should I pay you more when they charge less?"*

What three specific quantifiable Benefits will you use to prove your value to this particular Buyer?

1)

2)

3)

E. *"Why should I switch from the vendor I know?"*

What three **Status Quo Probes** will you use to set up a discussion of differentiating points between you and the competition?

1)

2)

3)

What Buyer's **commitment** would you like to achieve?

What **Objections** will you most likely hear from this Buyer?

Develop your Answers to those **Objections** including **Proof Statements**:

What **Closes** will you most likely use?

                                        ©Vass 2010-2021

Pre-Presentation Checklist

Physical setup for the Presentation:

Where will this presentation take place?

What is the shape of the room?

How will be room be arranged?

What kind of media equipment will be in the room? (Overhead projector, slide projector, blackboard, flip chart, video, on-line, Zoom, etc)?

People in the Presentation:

Who will be attending from the Buyer's side?

What is each of their responsibilities?

What is each of their interests in the meeting?

Why is your company going to attend?

Expectations of the Presentation:

What are you expecting to see and hear from your company? or

What are you expecting to have your company cover during this meeting?

What kind of an outcome would you like to see from this meeting in the short term (1 week)? Long term (30 days)?

What are the most important issues for us to address during this meeting?

How do we measure success?

What do you expect your company to do for/with you as the next step following the presentation?

Objectives of Presentation

What intermediate Buyer commitments, if any, will be available to close on?

The Next Sale

The objective of this exercise is two-fold:

1) to develop a presentation incorporating tactics you have learned in Soft Selling in a Hard World.

2) to help you close an upcoming important sale.

Choose a new business deal you will call on within 60 days that is qualified in several of the following ways:

- you have never called on them before,
- you are still in the initial stages of contact,
- they called you, most likely to perform their due diligence,
- it is a large enough opportunity to be profitable for both you and your company,
- it currently does business with the competition or,
- are not currently using your services and should be

If you have several opportunities to choose from, choose the most challenging one.

If you sell as a team you may prepare as a team, however, you will execute the role play individually

PLEASE PRINT CLEARLY YOUR ANSWERS TO THE FOLLOWING QUESTIONS:

Write enough information so you don't have to over-explain the situation at role play time.

Name of Company?
What does this Company do?
Is this a publicly traded company?

Your contact's position or business title in the company?

What do you know that motivates you to call on this account now?

What has prevented your firm from selling everything it wants to this client?

What is your contact most interested in achieving for his/her company?

What is the contact most interested in achieving for him/herself?

©Vass 2010-2021

The Next Sale (continued)

What will you sell to this client?

What is the total dollar value of this sale?

What concerns or objections do you anticipate they might have?

What else do you know about this client or this contact that will influence this sale?

(If this company currently does business with you, answer questions A through E)
A) How long has this company (or prospect) done business with your firm?

B) What services do they buy now?

C) This client's approximate annual purchases of your firm's services?

D) What problems have you encountered with this client?

E) What is the contact's perception of your firm?

(If this company currently does business with your competitor, answer questions F and G)

F) What competitors' services do they use now?

G) What are the client's approximate annual purchases of competitor's services?

Vass Fee Defense (Prove your value)

(1) OUR FEE = $_____

(2) THEIR FEE = $_____

(3) FEE DIFFERENCE = $_____

Our Unique FEATURES	Our Unique BENEFITS	Add dollar Value over Competition

Total Value of our UNIQUE BENEFITS $_____

DIVIDED BY

Fee Difference (from line 3)　　　　$_____

EQUALS

Return on Investment　　　_____%

　　　　©Vass 2010-2021

Voice Mail

Businesses now use electronic trash filters called voice mail, a blessing if you are already doing business with a Client, a curse if you aren't.

Voice mail is a useful selling tool. When leaving a message on a Client's voice mail, a slight change of tactics works well. Leave your name, Mission Statement containing a compelling Benefit, and a Proof Statement. (Studies show that for men, leaving only your name and phone number has an impossibly low return call success rate, perhaps 10% or less in some market. Women often have their calls returned 100% of the time if they leave their name. In addition, our research found that leaving only a Mission Statement resulted in 20% of calls being returned. Leaving a Mission Statement with a Proof Statement resulted in 70% call-backs. As in:

"This is Jesse Claymore of ExecSkills. Our business is helping companies reduce recruiting costs by 42%, or more, and still maintain control of the process. Using our services, Cona Cola was able to cut the costs of a project by $212,000. Kimster Clark was able to cut costs on a project by $155,000.

Please give me a call at 1-800-JESSE to see how we may be able to cut costs on your next recruiting project."

The Gatekeeper

Sometimes the toughest part of telephone work is getting by the gatekeeper. Often, if a Seller is polite and respectful, the gatekeeper can be enlisted to help you speak to the executive he or she protects.

Many voice mail systems will switch you to a living person if you touch "0" during the Client's recorded greeting. Establish if that living person is a remote receptionist or the Client's assistant. If it's the receptionist, locate the Client's assistant and then sell him or her as if your success depends on it, because it does.

Start with a Mission Statement and state what you need adjusted for the assistant personally, that is, make the assistant an important contributor to his or her organization's profits, etc. Make an appointment to call that assistant when the target person is in. Then email a short introduction to the assistant thanking him or her for taking the time to speak with you and confirming the telephone appointment.

©Vass 2010-2021

Gatekeeper Appointment

At the appointed time, you can then start the presentation to the assistant by saying, "You asked me to call you back at this time to speak with Jack Black. Is this a convenient time?" Usually they will put you through. Treat gatekeepers nicely; they are influence brokers.

The Full Sequence:

- Call during normal business hours. Calling in hopes the gatekeeper is away (before or after the normal business day) is an old gimmick and is mostly non-productive due to its abuse and "Caller ID" technology.
- Press "0" to leave the decision-maker's mailbox. It will take you to the switchboard or the decision-maker's Assistant. If you reach the switchboard, ask to speak to the Assistant.
- Since Assistants are hired for their intelligence and organizational skills, they often arrange the decision-maker's schedule, meetings, flights, lodgings, collect and screen E-mail and voice mail messages, and manage other aspects of their boss's business and personal life. Sometimes they have signing power, as well.
- Sell the Assistant as if he or she is the president. Start with a personalized Mission Statement and probe to find the ideal time to call the decision maker to discuss how other firms have achieved the benefits you sell.
- After establishing the ideal time to call again, be sure you get the Assistant's name, title, extension number and fax number. If it is awkward to get it from the Assistant directly, call the switchboard at the main number to get the information.
- Immediately after hanging up, fax your own version of the conversation attached.
- At the appointed time, call the Assistant, not the decision maker. Remind him or her that you are calling at the suggested time and ask if it is a convenient time to speak to the decision maker. If not, have the Assistant suggest a more suitable time.

In Summary:

- Sell to the assistant, not as a gatekeeper but as if he or she is president of the company.
- Close on the ideal time to speak with the decision maker for ten minutes (or less).
- Confirm the Assistant's email, mailing address, fax numbers, etc. either with the Assistant or the switchboard.
- Fax boiler plate letter (sample on next page)
- Call the Assistant at the appointed time

   ©Vass 2010-2021

Sample Email to Decision-Maker's Assistant

Computer Data Corporation
279 Software Park
Toledo OH 20345

<u>Attn: Ms. Mary Right, Secretary to the President</u>

Dear Ms. Right,

Thank you for taking the time to speak with me this morning.

As we discussed, with the confusing choices of (widgets) now available, making an informed and correct decision reflects directly on you and your company.

The ABC Company provides (widgets/solutions) that (increase/reduce/save) (software publishers) like (Computer Data Corporation) as much as (42% in network management costs).

The CEO of Bartok Mainframes, Mr. Robert Bartok, wrote:

> *"ABC's Widget IV helps us save over 40% in administrator and user related personnel costs, allowing us to invest the savings in growing our core business."*

A 2010 Gartner Group study also found that Widget IV customers reduced their real networking costs by 73%.

As you suggest, Ms. Right, I will call you August 6 at 9:00 AM to set up a meeting with Mr. Bob Jones to discuss how other computer companies have converted networking savings to increased market share.

I look forward to speaking with you then.

Yours truly,

Sharon Smith, Network Specialist
ABC Company

Proof Statement Letter

Mr. Blene Foonman, Vice President Ageless Software,
234 Silicon Parkway,
Anytown, CA 92111

Dear Sir,

Thank you for your time today. As discussed, Pan Dowdy Computers is working to gain a better understanding of how our clients have increased sales or revenue, saved time, reduced administrative costs, etc. by utilizing our products.

As a valued customer, we would consider it a privilege to use you as a business reference. It would be greatly appreciated if you would take one minute to confirm the comments you made in our telephone conversation.

With your kind permission, we may selectively and discreetly use your comments in our future public relations efforts.

You mentioned that,
"PanDowdy Computers has helped you reduce your computer support costs by 65%, saving you 1,160 hours of labor or about $45,000"

If this correctly summarizes what we discussed, simply confirm below that you are comfortable with the contents and fax it back to me. If you wish, please edit or modify your quote in the space provided, either handwritten or typed. This doesn t have to be a Shakespearean masterpiece, the more straightforward and candid the better.

My fax number is (214) 555-5555
Email: jcork@acmemail.com
Thanks for your help.

Jenny Cork,
Marketing Manager PanDowdy Computers

Sample Follow-up Letter

Dear Sir or Madam,

Thank you for the opportunity to discuss how Acme Computers helps declavinator manufacturers increase revenues by 22% or more.

Our discussion today indicated that among your critical concerns were:

1. delinquent receivables due to lack of immediate credit information

2. 35 customer complaints per week concerning slow order shipping

3. $10,000 in weekly catalog publication costs

Acme's solution to these problems:

1. gives you immediate access to credit information and control of receivables

2. provides daily order entry which reduces turnaround time by 30%

3. publishes an online catalog to create incremental savings of $520,000 per year

Mr. Robert Sanchez, CEO of Sanchez Swatter Corporation, manufacturers of the famous "Muerta Fly" brand writes,

> *"Within three months, Acme's laptop order system*
> *reduced our outstanding receivables from 94 to 45 days."*

Other manufacturers' experiences confirm these results.

I look forward to our meeting on October 5 and to helping you exceed your sales and revenue targets next year and beyond.

Cordially,

Nigel Furn
Sales Representative

ACKNOWLEDGEMENTS

This guide is the collective knowledge of Howard Camber, Iris Herrin and Jerry Vass—the VASS© partners/classroom trainers. Their skill teaching 12,000 high-end salespeople in hard-core boot-camps made their students millions.

Thanks to all our clients who entrusted us with the creative minds of their most valuable business assets—the salespeople who create the cash flow. They are the solitary warriors who walk naked into the business arena each day, choke down their fear and carry the weight of their firm on their shoulders.

VASS®

1093 A1a Beach Boulevard #448
Saint Augustine, FL 32080
vass@vass.com

 ©Vass 2010-2021

Printed in Great Britain
by Amazon

37408950R00031